WonderWorks

Decodable Reader

Unit 3

McGraw Hill

Contents

Around
Dad's Ranch
by David Baker
illustrated by Meryl Henderson
1

Safe Snakes
by Melissa Meyers
9

Time to Pick Up Together
by Camille Iglesias
illustrated by Anni Matsick
17

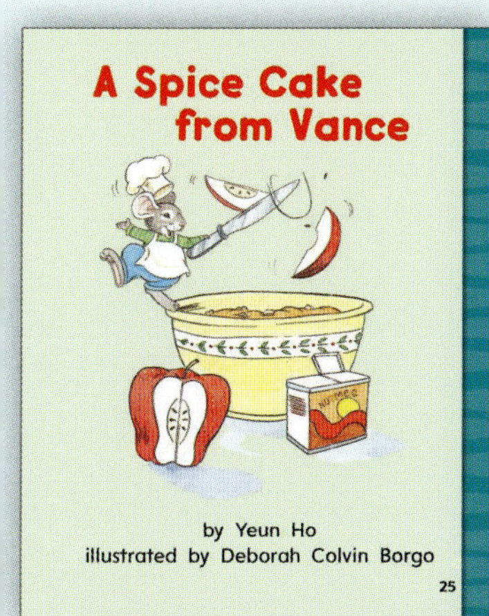
A Spice Cake from Vance
by Yeun Ho
illustrated by Deborah Colvin Borgo
25

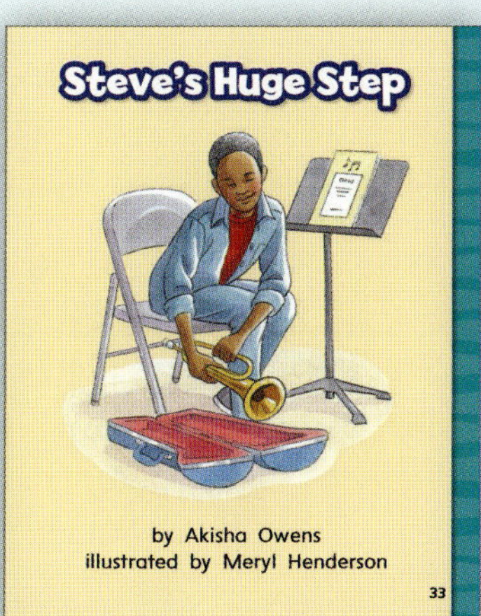
Steve's Huge Step
by Akisha Owens
illustrated by Meryl Henderson
33

Around Dad's Ranch

by David Baker

illustrated by Meryl Henderson

This is Mitch.
Mitch's Dad has a ranch.
It is a big **place**.

Dad has a truck.
Dad has a van.
Mitch helps Dad hitch the van.
Many chicks peck in a pen.

Mitch and Dad will go out.
Mitch checks his chicks.
Mitch will not bring them.

Look at the truck!
It is stuck in a ditch!
Mitch must fetch Big Phil.

Mitch will **walk** Phil **around**.
Big Phil tugs and tugs.
The truck moves inch **by** inch.
Big Phil did it!

Big Phil likes to munch.
Big Phil gets a snack.
Big Phil is the best!

Safe Snakes

Mark Lehigh/Alamy

by Melissa Meyers

Alexander Gabrysch/Picture Press/Getty Images

Stephen Kirkpatrick/America 24-7/Getty Images

What helps a snake to be safe? A snake can't run. It does not have legs. What can a snake do?

Alexander Gabrysch/Picture Press/Getty Images

Snakes can make safe nests. A snake can dig a den in sand. It will nest in logs and under plants, too.

Snakes can get **away** fast. **Now** and then, a snake will slip under a rock. Then it can't be spotted.

Michael Sewell Visual Pursuit/Oxford Scientific/Getty Images

Some snakes have scales that blend in. They look the same as land. Scales help snakes move.

Andy Hunger/age footstock

Snakes can huff and hiss. A snake can shake at one end. A snake can flop and act as if it is dead.

Why is this snake safe **today**? It can escape. It can blend in. It can make its **way** to a safe spot.

Time to Pick Up Together

by Camille Iglesias
illustrated by Anni Matsick

This spot has lots of trash.
Let's pick it up **together**.
Then it will look **pretty**.

This is a bit of a bike.
No one can ride with it.
It will fit in a wide bag.

I will fill this bag.
I will pick up plates and cups tossed on the **green** grass.
My bag is filled with trash.

This is a smashed kite.
This is a white pipe.
We **should** pick them up
and toss them in the bag.

The trash is in a big pile.
A truck will pick it up.
The truck will drive it away.

This spot is pretty.
Grass can **grow**.
Kids can ride by the **water**.
Good job, kids!

A Spice Cake from Vance

by Yeun Ho

illustrated by Deborah Colvin Borgo

Once **upon** a time, Vance wished to bake his best cake. It was not just **any** cake. It was a fresh spice cake!

Vance placed his white
hat on his head.
He rested on the edge.
He added spice **from** a box.

Next, Vance chopped nuts.
He diced nine dates.
He added nuts and dates!

Vance danced on the edge.
Then he sliced and diced.
He added fresh things.
His cake looked quite good.

Vance mixed and mixed.
Then he got his cake mix in its pan.
The next stage was baking.

Then Vance iced his cake.
He cut a nice slice.
It was a good cake.
Vance felt **so happy**!

whiteboard

globe

Did you find?

book

ruler

Spot is published by Amicus Learning, an imprint of Amicus
P.O. Box 227, Mankato, MN 56002
www.amicuspublishing.us

Library of Congress Cataloging-in-Publication Data
Names: Golkar, Golriz, author.
Title: Teachers / by Golriz Golkar.
Description: Mankato, MN : Amicus Learning, [2026] | Series: Spot community helpers | Audience: Ages 4–7 | Audience: Grades K-1 | Summary: "Teachers teach reading, STEM, and more. Learn how they help their students in this low-level beginning reader that reinforces new vocabulary with a search-and-find feature. A great early social studies book that will inspire kindergartners and first graders to learn about jobs in their community"– Provided by publisher.
Identifiers: LCCN 2024043697 (print) | LCCN 2024043698 (ebook) | ISBN 9798892004930 (library binding) | ISBN 9798892005470 (paperback) | ISBN 9798892006019 (ebook)
Subjects: LCSH: Teachers–Juvenile literature. | Teaching–Juvenile literature.
Classification: LCC LB1775 .G645 2026 (print) | LCC LB1775 (ebook) | DDC 371.1–dc23/eng/20241010
LC record available at https://lccn.loc.gov/2024043697
LC ebook record available at https://lccn.loc.gov/2024043698

Ana Brauer, editor
Deb Miner, series designer
Sara Hood, book designer and photo researcher

Photos by Dreamstime/Monkey Business Images, cover; Getty Images/SDI Productions, 12–13, skynesher, 6-7; Shutterstock/Ljupco Smokovski, 1, Monkey Business Images, 4–5, PaniYani, 10–11, Rido, 3, SeventyFour, 8–9, wavebreakmedia, 14